THE 256 ODU OF IFA CUBAN AND TRADITIONAL VOL. 13
Òyèkú Ògúnda-Òyèkú Òsá

MARCELO MADAN

Copyright © 2009 Marcelo Madan
All rights reserved.
ISBN:
https://www.orunmilaeditio.com

NOTE TO THIS EDITION

As we have already noticed in our previous Ifá literatures, it is about transcription of manuscript documents, many of them unpublished, with different wording and literary styles, I have always tried to keep in essence, the idea of what was wanted to express, for Therefore, it is quite difficult to achieve uniformity of style in this regard. In this new presentation I show in each of the Odu, everything from the literature of Afro-Cuban Ifá and traditional African Ifá.

It is in my interest, to provide Ifá students this time, a broad vision in all its dimensions of what Ifá can encompass, taking into account, in addition, that what is presented in this is not everything, because Ifá is much deeper. and his literary work is much more abundant than what I show here, this is only a part, even when I have added to these volumes' concepts from the previously published ifá treatises, as well as traditional ifá. In addition, it is not my intention here to suggest any kind of supremacy between the two trends, only to show them as each of them is presented and that it is the reader himself who judges and prefers its future use. My aim is to offer you the possibility of having at hand, a renewed tool for study, broader and more effective that allows you at the same time, to enter the learning of both literatures without limitations or discrimination, each one in its field, because ultimately, the knowledge of Ifá is universal and is for everyone alike.

GRATEFULNESS

Thanks to Olodumare, for having enlightened me and allow to create this work, to be able to throw the light of knowledge to everyone who needs it.

Thanks to Orunmila spirit of light that guides me and takes me along the right path.

Thanks to Obatala, my guard angel who always accompanies me and provides timely protection.

Thanks to my maternal grandmother and godmother Rosa Torrez (Shangó Womí)

Thanks to my godfather Rubén Pineda Baba Ejiogbe

CONTENT

Chapter
1 OYEKU OGUNDA.................... Pag. 1
    Ifá de:
    Proverbs
    Born
    Brand
    Signalize
    Ifa Says
    Prohibitions
    Recommendations
    Ewé of Odu
    Pataki relationship
    Works
    Pataki or Stories
2 TRADITIONAL IFÁ OYEKU OGUNDA............................... Pag. 15
3 OYEKU OSA............................. Pag. 43
    Ifa de
    Proverbs
    Born
    Brand
    Signalize
    Ifa Says
    Prohibitions
    Recommendations
    Ewé of Odu
    Pataki relationship
    Works
    Pataki or Stories
4 TRADITIONAL IFÁ OYEKU OSA... Pag. 57
5 VOCABULARY AND DEFINITIONS Pag. 79

CHAPTER 1

ÒYÈKÚ ÒGÚNDÁ or TEKUNDA

```
    +
I   O
I   O
I   O
O   O
```

I PRAY:

Òyèkú Tekunda lobína nasá oyó opa otá kukú wo ra A dífá fún Abere we lubá Omo Òrúnmìlà koba ogun titi wo bebe ré olo tura agogo la bin Ikú teniyé Ewé Ogumá ifá ni òtá ojoojo Ebo adié eku èyé owó tete boru.

IFÁ OF:

• Ká fírè fún Obàtàlá, Òṣùn àti Òrúnmìlà.

PROVERBS:

• He who speaks slander of others lowers his own prestige

- A man may regret his previous actions, but he has to bear their consequences
- The tormentor makes his victims unyielding.
- The fire in the fields does not afflict the pigeon, because as soon as it sees the flames spreading, it goes to a shelter.

BORN:

- The spirituality of Ifá, is the spirit of Òrúnmìlà personified, it is its spiritual personification.
- The mensú (Jar loaded with the garment)
- The blowing otín chewed with ataare méta to the 4 winds in the Ìkokò of Òsányin.

BRAND

- In Ifá the arrival of the river

IFA

SIGNALIZE

- Sending witchcraft
- That they can poison you.

IFÁ SPEAKS

- That you can't be greedy because greed loses
- The spirituality of Ifá
- That with the same witchcraft the enemy is overcome

- That Awo can't go anywhere leaving his pending because he loses insurance
- To give Adié méjì to Òṣùn and take them to the river raw or cooked, as she determines
- Going to the field and luck in it and that you will find an Ọbìrin that will be your happiness
- To be satisfied so that you do not lose everything
- Of three enemies who do not wish good for you.
- To be careful with Àṣelú and to have to flee and hide
- Of Slander
- That the Awo must always have a tie in his pocket to throw him into what he eats when the place is not trustworthy because they can poison him. He will tie up any witchcraft they give the Awo
- From poisoning by enemies with whom one shares
- From three people who advise you badly to harm and create conflicts
- Of one thing that can happen that people will be amazed
- That if they send for him from the field, it is for something good

PROHIBITIONS

- You can't leave the safe for the doubtful
- Do not eat spicy
- Do not drink dry wine
- You can't be greedy

RECOMMENDATIONS

- Give two hens to Òṣùn and take them to the river
- Be compliant, do not lose everything
- Beware of a slander
- Give Canistel to Òṣùn
- Prepare an Iṣé de Òsányin with a mirror

EWÉ ODÙ ÒYÈKÚ ÒGÚNDÁ

Hierba la Niña----Bejuco Berraco

PATAKI LISTING

1. Loa three liars or aráyé de Òrúnmìlà
2. The Stevedore
3. The four Winds
4. The dog lost the Gandinga because of greedy
5. The sack and the Serpent
6. Ọbàtàlá and salt

WORKS WITH ÒYÈKÚ ÒGÚNDÁ

Ẹbọ: A rooster, gandinga and dog

Gandinga

Ẹbọ: Òbúko, Àkúko, Osaidie, adié méjì, Ẹiyelé méjì, malaguidí méta, Èbìtì méta, Gbogbo Leniya, Àṣe, Igi, inlé Onika, ọ̀pọ̀lọ̀pọ̀ owó.

Note: Òbúko for Òṣùn, Àkúko for Èṣù, Osaidie opa wodo, Ẹiyelé méjì for Ọbàtàlá.

Ẹbọ: A Rooster, atitan ilé loya, eku, eja, epo, ọ̀pọ̀lọ̀pọ̀ owó.

<u>In the Odù Ọ̀yẹ̀kú Funda</u>

It is dedicated to the protective Eegún, in a hollow tree in the forest, brandy, coffee, water, flowers, and a tobacco with a candle.

Elégbàra is given a small mirror washed with omiero and a gio-gio is fed from the back together with Elégbàra.

Òrúnmìlà is given a little mirror and a piece of Caña Brava Take bone marrow broth with an Iwereyeye.

On an empty stomach, a glass of otin is taken to stimulate

Caña Brava (Bamboo)

He goes to the foot of a Caña Brava bush, takes a tip of a branch, puts it on his stomach and releases it, asking Olófin, Òṣùn and Òrúnmìlà, to take away the bad. Here the gandinga speaks.

The Ikofá is put in front of a Caña Brava joint.

For this Ifá, a hand of 16 Dilogún washed in a tureen is placed in front of the Ifá of the Awó.

Ẹbọ: A rooster, gandinga and Dog.

Ẹbọ: Òbúko, Àkúko, Osaidie, adie méjì, ẹiyelé méjì, malaguidí méta, Èbìtì méta, Gbogbo Leniya, àṣe, igi, Inlé Onika, opolopo owó.

Note:

Òbúko for òṣùn, àkúko for Èṣù, osaidie opa guodo, ẹiyelé méjì for Òbàtála.

It is born: The spirituality of Ifá is the spirit of Òrúnmìlà personified, it is his spiritual personification.

IFA

ÒYÈKÚ TEKUNDA PÀTAKI 1 " THE THREE ARAYÉ OF ÒRÚNMÌLÀ"

I PRAY

Akuata Bo Ami Amu Okete Mosu Soyo Oṣe Lo Otín Lose Aun Ota Òrúnmìlà Olófin Dire Ife Lo Opa Òrúnmìlà.

ẸBọ: Òbúko, Àkúko, Osaidie méjì, ẹiyelé méjì, malaguidí méta, èbìtì.

Distribution:

Òbúko for Òṣùn, Àkúko for Èṣù, Osaidie for Paraldo, ẹiyelé méjì for Olófin or Òbàtála (ask if the adie méjì are given jointly to Òṣùn and Òrúnmìlà).

Ifá ni Káfírèfún Òṣùn, Lodafún Olófin, Adífáfún Èṣù.

Pàtaki

Olofin sent for Òrúnmìlà to go to the land of Ife, because there were many dead and they wanted to see what was done to avoid this.

When Òrúnmìlà left his house, he met one who told him that if he was going to the land of Ife, he should not do it, because he had heard a bad conversation regarding him. Òrúnmìlà continued on his way and when he was going through the middle of the town, another came who told him that if he was going to the land of Ifá that he should not go, because they were waiting for him and preparing a trap to catch him. Òrúnmìlà did not pay attention to him either and continued on his way, but when he was at the exit of the town, another came and told him not to go to Ife, because they were waiting for him to kill him. This time Òrúnmìlà did get scared and instead of following his path, he fled to the mountain and hid in a hollow stick, so that no one would see him. Time passed and he already knew that people were looking for him, when a pregnant woman appeared, who went to the mountain every day, to look for firewood, to sell and when she saw the hollow stick where Òrúnmìlà was, she thought it was easier for her cut it down and headed for it. When she took the first swing, she heard them sing; The woman stood still and heard the same song again and thought about who it would be, when she gave the second blow, she heard the song again and said to herself, that is Òrúnmìlà, she looked inside the tree and saw him, asking him what he was doing there, I am hiding because they say they are going to kill me, answered Òrúnmìlà, no sir, on the contrary, people are very sad because they don't see it. He gives her the food she was carrying and asks her to wait for him, that she would be right back. She left and went to the King's house informing him that he had found Òrúnmìlà. If it's true, I'm going to give you all the wealth you want, but right now you're going to look for it, he answered her and gave her assistants to accompany her; she returned to the place where Òrúnmìlà was hidden and brought him to the presence of the King, who asked her why he had not come when Olofin had sent for him. Òrúnmìlà paused and then added; To answer you correctly I need you to send me to look for the goat, the rooster and the dove first, which were the reason why I did not come. The goat told me that they were waiting for me to kick Ogun out. The rooster told me that they were going to kill me and the dove that there was a trap. That's why I got scared and hid. From today, all of you will serve for Ẹbọ and to eat, said Olófin, addressing the three liars, the goat will be eaten by Òṣùn and the pigeon will be eaten by me and Òrúnmìlà, he kept the woman, the riches and the servants.

Note:

He says Ifá that there are three people who advise him badly to harm him and create conflicts. Be careful with one thing that is going to happen to you and people are going to be shocked. They're going to send you out of the fields to look for you, a berry that's part of something good.

ÒYÈKÚ TEKUNDA PÀTAKI 2 "THE STEVEDORE"

I PRAY:

Intorí ẹiyelé ni lete awo ibasun bowó no lolo ero lomba tumba awo ẹiyelé ni adífáfún tobo ṣiri Ifá Òbúko odunde aṣọ teledi intorí ọkọnrin ile lona, Lodafún Òbàtála.

Ẹbọ: 1 Rooster, atitan ilé loya, eku, eja, epo, opolopo owó

Pàtaki

There was a man who worked in the square and was a stevedore in it and he did errands for Òrúnmìlà, where one day, Òbàtála saw him after he had long received the hand of Ifá (Owo fo kan), where he called Òbàtála the attention seeing him work as a stevedore in the square, having received Ifá and told him to tell Òrunla, that he was not using him as an errand boy, nor that he was loading things in the square. After hearing Òbàtála, he went to Òrunla and told him what happened when he found Òbàtála, Òrúnmìlà told him to tell Òbàtála that he did not send him to do that job, nor did he force him, where The man told Òbàtála, because he believed that it was more useful that way, where Òbàtála told him, well, then you will always continue to be a charger.

ÒYÈKÚ TEKUNDA PÀTAKI 3 "THE FOUR WINDS"

Ẹbọ:

Osaidie méjì, obí atare marun, èbìtì, malaguidí, atitan ilé, ewéfá gbogbo igi eku, eja, epo, àgbado, opolopo owó.

Note:

Before starting the Ẹbọ, the person will chew a small piece of obí with ataré méta or marun and pour it all into the Ẹbọ.

Distribution:

Osaidie for Ẹbọ Paraldo. Osaidie for Òsányin with gbogbo igi to defeat the enemy.

Nota:

Here is born the blowing of the obí to the 4 winds when Òsányin is done, the Awó of this sign will always have to be with a tie in his pockets to throw everything he eats when the place is not trustworthy, because they want to poison him. The atare disrupts any sorcery given to the Awo.

Pàtaki

On this road there was a town where an Awo lived who had many Awoses enemies, these araye also did not know how they were going to liquidate him, because they had already done everything to him and they could not with him, both with spiritual and material works. One day, they invite him to a plant to poison him, but the Awo had become osode and this Ifá came out, which told him that the ataaré disrupted any witchcraft they gave the Awo, it disintegrated it. The Awo carried ataaré in his pockets and when he arrived at the plant, the other Awoses who had prepared the trap for him, immediately sent him to give coconut to Òsányin, because the poison was in the coconuts, but what would not be the astonishment of the enemies, seeing that the Awo put in the little piece of obi that he took to chew, I will tie méta and then they said. "The truth is that with him we can't."

ÒYÈKÚ TEKUNDA PÀTAKI 4 "THE DOG LOST GANDINGA (VISCERAS) BECAUSE OF GREEDY"

Pàtaki

One time, a dog stole some viscera from a slaughterhouse, ran away and ran nonstop and when he was going to cross the river, in the reflection of the water, he saw a viscera larger than the one he was carrying in his mouth, he immediately dropped the that he was carrying, to pick up the one he had seen that was more voluminous and it fell into the water, losing the image, and because of his greed he was left without one and without the other.

Note: Avoid being greedy.

ÒYÈKÚ TEKUNDA PÀTAKI 5 "THE SACK AND THE SERPENT"

Pàtaki

Ifá says that Òbàtála was going to make a trip to the countryside, but first, he wanted to know what Òrúnmìlà was saying to him, he told him to do Ẹbọ before leaving for that trip, because he was going to have problems with the law. Òbàtála said that he was very important and that he was not going to do it and he took a sack, two coconuts, a rope and left.

In a place where he had to jump over an obstacle, he abandoned the sack at one end and jumped on the other side, but the enemy who lay in wait for him hidden, opened the sack and threw a snake at him, Òbàtála did not see him and reloaded his sack, but the child, son of the enemy, saw the sack and put his hand in and the snake bit him.

The police arrested Òbàtála and on the way they began to investigate, who threw the snake in the sack, which they could not find out, but Òbàtála went to Òrúnmìlà and he told him that the father was to blame for what had happened to him. boy and Òbàtála was acquitted for his innocence and had to do Ẹbọ with a sack, a rope and two coconuts.

ÒYÈKÚ TEKUNDA PÀTAKI 6 "OBATALA AND SALT"

Pàtaki

Òbàtála never went outside and everything that was cooked in the house was without salt. But one day, Òbàtála prepared a trip, but he entrusted his trusted servant that he could give the food to all the other servants with salt. But as it was customary to cook without salt, the servant forgot to add salt to the food, as Òbàtála had ordered. This was enough for the other servants to turn around and prepare a lot of gossip for Òbàtála when he returned.

Then the servant knowing what awaited him, went to Òrúnmìlà's house, so that he would defend him from that difficulty and Èṣù took charge of adding what he lacked. When Òbàtála arrived, he tried the food and could not believe anything that his servants told him.

ORISHA OSUN

CHAPTER 2

TRADITIONAL IFA ÒYÈKÚ ÒGÚNDÀ

(ÒYEKU OJOMOODA; ÒYEKU EGUNTAN; ÒYEKU OJONDA; ÒYEJU OJOODA)

ÒYÈKÚ ÒGÚNDÀ VERSE 1

Aworan wo'ni peete-peete

Dia fun Ojomooda

Tii se omo Ajaniwarun

Ebo ni won ni ko waa se

O gb'ebo, o ru'bo

Ojo ti mo da ee pe o

Igunyan orun ee gun o

Iroko orun ee ro

Ipoko orun ee po

Oyeku ojomooda

Ko nii je ki nmese mi rorun o

Translation

A carved image looked at one without any expression

Ifá's message for Ojomooda

Ajaniwarun's son

He was advised to offer ebo

fulfilled

My appointed date is not reached

The sky yam pound hadn't started banging

And the heaven preparer yam flour had not begun its preparation

The cornmeal preparer from heaven had not started the preparation of the meal

Oyeku-Ojomooda,

Will not allow me to experience and premature death

PROPHECY

1. Ifá says that long life is foreseen for you. Ifa assures you that you will not die young, and you will be able to see the birth and growth of your children and grandchildren. Ifa advises you to offer ebo with a mature sheep and money.

ÒYÈKÚ ÒGÚNDÀ VERSE 2

Owo ti eni mo

Oun ni eni nse

Dia fun Babarinde

Omo adebiti sola

Ebo ni won ni ko waa se

O gb'ebo, o ru'bo

Oun ti mo mo

Ni e je nse

Babarinde o de o

Omo adebiti sola

Translation

The business that is understood

That's what one has to do

Ifá's message for Babarinde

The one who sets the traps and made himself prosperous

He was advised to offer ebo

fulfilled

business i understand

That's what you need for me to do

Here comes Babarinde

The one who sets the traps and made himself prosperous

PROPHECY

2. Ifá says that he is going to stand out in the field of marketing, commercial banking, security, military or paramilitary, fields. Ifa advises you not to allow anyone to introduce a profession for you again. Rather, he has to go to the profession that he understands very well. Ifa advises you to offer ebo with four pigeons and money.

ÒYÈKÚ ÒGÚNDÀ VERSE 3

Oyeku ojoooda gbaragada

O ro po onyagbe

Dia fun Akosimoba

Ti nfekun sunrahun omo

Ebo ni won ni ko waa se

O gb'ebo, o ru'bo

Akosimoba ma nkomoo rete o

E wa womo yooyo leyin Akosi

Translation

Oyeku ojoooda gbaragada

O ro po onyagbe

Ifá's message for Akosimoba

When crying, lamenting her inability to receive the blessing of the fruit of the womb

She was advised to offer ebo

she obeyed

Akosimoba is taking her children to her nest

Come and see many children behind Akosi

PROPHECY

3. Ifá says that you will be blessed with many children in life. If for some reason her spouse experiences the problem of procreation there is no need for you to offer ebo with four rats, four fish, one hen, one mature goat and money. The goat will be slaughtered and its reproductive organ will be removed and cooked with Eyin-Olobe leaves. She also has to tie the Ifa necklace three days after offering this ebo.

ÒYÈKÚ ÒGÚNDÀ VERSE 4

Eeyan lo wa leyin osa

Ko too ma je aarokun

Dia fun Ojoooda

A figba akara sete

Ebo ni won ni ko waa se

O gb'ebo, o ru'bo

Ota awo lo sorun

Bi akara ba wonu epo

Okiki a ta gee

Translation

Eeyan lo wa Leyin osa

Ko too ma je aarokun

Ifa's message for Ojooda

Who uses 200 Akara balls to overcome conspiracies

She was advised to offer ebo

fulfilled

All enemies of Awo go to heaven

Every time he enters the hot oil palm Akara

The noise was heard throughout

PROPHECY

4. Ifa assures you that you will be victorious over all your enemies. Ifá says that no matter how many there are, all of them will regret their actions. As a matter of fact, Ifá says that many of the enemies of it, who taste this Akara that you need to prepare will experience premature death. Ifa advises you to offer ebo with 200 Akara balls, 2 chickens and money. Iyerosun is sprinkled on the Ifá tray and Oyeku Ogundá will

be stamped on it. This particular verse will be recited and then the Iyerosun is poured over Akara. After this, the Akara will be shared among everyone around you.

ÒYÈKÚ ÒGÚNDÀ VERSE 5

Oye guda-guda-guda

Dia fun Ojoooda

Tii somo bibi inu Agbonniregun

Ebo ni won ni ko waa se

O gb'ebo, o ru'bo

Ko le se o

Ko le ye

Itadogun Awo ko ni ye o

Ko le se o

Ko le ye

Itadogun awo kii ye o

Translation

Hey guda-guda-guda

Ifá's message for Ojoooda

The son of Agbonniregun

He was advised to offer ebo

fulfilled

You can not lose

can't be postponed

The Periodic Itadogun of Awo

can't be postponed

PROPHECY

5. Ifa advises you to observe the periodic Ose of Ifa regularly. Ifá says that doing this will cause all his prayers to be answered by Olodumare and all the Irunmole. Ifa assures you that you will succeed where others have failed. Ifa advises you to offer ebo with four rats, four fish, two pigeons, two hens, two guinea fowl, two roosters and money. It is also necessary to feed Ifa with two rats and two fish.

ÒYÈKÚ ÒGÚNDÀ VERSE 6

Opon lopon ide

Iroke niroke Orunmila

Dia fun Ojomooda

Ti won nfojo iku re da piiti

Ebo ni won ni ko waa se

O gb'ebo, o ru'bo

Orunmila ni to ba se pe bi ise omo toun ba ni o

Igunyan orun koi gun

Iroka orun koi ro

Oyeku-ojoooda o nii je nmise mi gborun

Aso ni mo fi ran won

Aguntan ni mo fi to o

Translation

The tray is made with bronze

And the Iroke is the collector of Orunmila

Ifá's message for Ojomooda

When they were counting it's day to go back to heaven

She was advised to offer ebo

fulfilled

Orunmila declared that if it were to be her own son that they refer to

The sky yam pounds hadn't started pounding

And the meal preparer yam in heaven had not started his preparation

Oyeku-Ojooda won't let me go to heaven early

It comes to dress that she had sent to them

And I followed with a matured sheep

PROPHECY

6. Ifá says that you will be protected against death, affliction, contention and loss. Ifa says that his heavenly peers are eager to bring him back to heaven, but this will not happen quickly if you offer ebo. Ifa advises you to offer ebo with: a mature sheep, a bundle of white clothing, a bunch of palm oil and money.

ÒYÈKÚ ÒGÚNDÀ VERSE 7

Eta-kankan Babalawo Agbe

Lo dia fun Agbe

Won ni ki Agbe o sebo

Ko le baa gberi igi dale

Eta-sasa, Babalawo Aluko

Lo dia fun Aluko

Won ni ki Aluko sebo

Ko le baa gbe'ri igi dale

Bagbe ba ke

Egbe re a ke

Baluko ba ke

Egbe re a gba

Translation

Eta Kankan, the Babalawo of Agbe, the blue touraco

Launched Ifá for Agbe

Agbe advised to offer ebo

To give him long life on top of the tree

Eta sasa, the Babalawo of Aluko the brown touraco

Launched Ifá for Aluko

Aluko advised to offer ebo

In order to live long at the top of the tree

both meet

If Agbe screams

All his colleagues chorus his cry

And if Aluko quirks

All his contemporaries will support him

PROPHECY

7. Ifa advises you to offer ebo and feed Egbe regularly. Ifá says that doing this will give you support and advance more than you can imagine in life. Ifa advises you to offer ebo with four guinea fowl, four pigeons and money. After this he has to find out what his Egbe will take from you and give to them accordingly.

ÒYÈKÚ ÒGÚNDÀ VERSE 8

Eyo fuu mariwo

Dia fun Ooto

Ti ntoru bo waye

Ebo ni won ni ko waa se

O gb'ebo, o ru'bo

Eyo fuu mariwo

A ti mu Ooto joye Aye o!

Translation

Eyo Fuu mariwó

Ifá's message for Ooto, Truth

If it comes from heaven to Earth

He was advised to offer ebo

fulfilled

Eyo Fuu mariwó

We have installed Otito with honor in this world

PROPHECY

8. Ifá says that you must always tell the truth at all times. Ifa, however, warns that it is a coin that he has in short supply. Ifá says that if this is the truth, you must change immediately and

start being absolutely honest and sincere in everything you do. Therein lies success, peace of mind, joy, elevation and self-actualization for you. Ifa advises you to offer ebo with two roosters, two hens and money.

ÒYÈKÚ ÒGÚNDÀ VERSE 9

Oyeku Ojoooda gbaragada loropo onyagbe

Dia fun Agbe Dudu

Tii somo Oye Oluigbo

Oyeku Ojoooda gbaragada loropo onyagbe

Dia fun Aluko Dodoodo

Tii somo Olosun Egan

Oyeku Ojoooda gbaragada loropo onyagbe

Dia fun Odidere mofe

Omo Odo-Oba

Omo atorun gbegba aje kari waye

Oyeku Ojoooda gbaragada loropo onyagbe

Dia fun Owawa

Tii somo ikeyin won lenjelenje

Ebo ni won ni ki won waa se

Owawa nikan nibe leyin ti nsebo

Meewa mo o iku ye, owawa

Meewa mo o ejo ye, owawa

Meewa mo o arun ye, owawa

Meewa mo o ija ye, owawa

Meewa mo o Arun vosotros, owawa

Meewa mo o ija vosotros, owawa

Translation

Oyeku Ojoooda gbaragada loropo onyagbe

Ifá's message for Agbe dark skin

The defending champion in the woods

Oyeku Ojoooda gbaragada loropo onyagbe

The Ifá message for the red-skinned Aluko

The owner of the plains

Oyeku Ojoooda gbaragada loropo onyagbe

Ifá's message for Odidere-Mofe, the Parrot

Odo-Oba's offspring

He who carries his gourd of wealth in the world

Oyeku Ojoooda gbaragada loropo onyagbe

Ifá's message for Owawa, The Bear Tree

Who is the youngest among them

They were advised to offer ebo

Only Owawa complied with the advice

I do not go anymore

Death had passed me by, Owawa

I do not go anymore

Affliction had missed me, Owawa

I do not go anymore

Containment had overlooked me, Owawa

I do not go anymore

Loss had passed me by, Owawa

PROPHECY

9. Ifá says that there is a tendency for your parents, especially your mother, to give birth to four children. Ifá says that every time there is going to be a ceremony that involves the four of you, you should check and cross-check with Ifa over and over again before doing that ceremony. If you are not sure of Ifá's response through any ceremony, please boycut this, the ceremony and please don't do it. If it is not possible for all four of you to stand for the ceremony, please make sure that all four of you are not attending the ceremony. Ifá advises each of you to offer ebo with two chickens, two guinea fowl, two roosters, and money. Each of you also have to feed Ifa with eight rats and eight fish.

ÒYÈKÚ ÒGÚNDÀ VERSE 10

Oori kannko

Dia fun Oori patako

Won ni ko ma dee omo re late

O koti ogbonyin sebo

Gbogbo isowo ope

Eni gbebo nbe ko wa sebo o

Gbogbo isowo ope

Translation

oori kanko

Launched Ifá for the giant Oori tree

She was advised not to wear a wide-brimmed hat for her children

She refused to comply

All Ifa devotees

That she advised them to offer ebo to comply accordingly

All Ifa followers

PROPHECY

10. Ifa warns you not to wear a wide hat in any condition. Ifá says that if you are in the habit of wearing a wide hat, you have

a chance of losing your children in the flower. Ifa advises you to offer ebo with two hens, two roosters and money.

ÒYÈKÚ ÒGÚNDÀ VERSE 11

Sakoto ile nii ba agbalagba leru

Dia fun Oyigidigbi

Ti nbe laarin ota

Ebo ni won ni ko waa se

O gb'ebo, o ru'bo

O ni laye la boke

Laye la o foke si

Translation

A deep ditch is that it gives a serious major apprehension

Ifá's message for Oyigidigbi

When I was in the midst of enemies

He advised to offer ebo

fulfilled

He declared that we find the hill in the world

And we'll get off the hill in this world

PROPHECY

11. Ifá says that he foresees victory for you. Ifa says that his destiny is such that many people will conspire to substantially harm or reduce, but all of them will fail. Ifá says that none of his antagonists or enemies will have the power to harm or reduce you. ifa advises you to offer ebo with a mature goat and money. It is also necessary to feed Oke in his case.

ÒYÈKÚ ÒGÚNDÀ VERSE 12

Angbadu awo oko

Yapayapa lo to aala a gba

Dia fun Orunmila

Ifa nsawo lo apa okun

Oun ilameji osa

O nlo gbagun iyun

O nlo gbagun ide

O nlo gbagun ologinninginni aso Irada

Ebo ni won ni ko waa se

O gb'ebo, o ru'bo

Ko pe, ko jinna

E wa ba ni ni jebutu ire gbogbo

Translation

Angbadu is the awo of agricultural land

Yapayapa what AALA a gba

Ifá's message for Orunmila

When you go on an Ifa mission to one side of the sea

And the other side of the lagoon

When I was going to bring the corals back home

And to make brass ornaments

And also to bring back high quality clothing

He was advised to offer ebo

fulfilled

In a short time, not far

Join us in the midst of all life Ire

PROPHECY

12. Ifá says that every time you are going to go on a long journey in order to transact your business or in the course of your professional vocation, there is a need for you to offer ebo in order to allow it to bring benefits and acknowledgment back home. Ifa advises you to offer ebo with two pigeons, two chickens and money.

ÒYÈKÚ ÒGÚNDÀ VERSE 13

13. Ifá says that the time in your life is approaching when you are faced with a life-threatening health problem. Ifa assures you that with proper ebo you will survive the disease. As a consequence, it is recommended that you offer this ebo even before the illness begins. Ifa advises you to offer ebo with 200 hoes, and 200 cloth spinners.

Omo olowo nii soso nii ro yebeyeb

Omo otosi nii gbaja deere kanle

Dia fun Ojomida

Omo Alapa mori

Omo ateni-lejeleje fori gbeji

Igbati n sogbogbo arun

Ti nnaji ati dide

Ebo ni won ni ko waa se

O gb'ebo, o ru'bo

Kinlo waa yeku Ojomida o

Igba oko, igba oko

Atori maa se belenje

Translation

The son of a rich person usually ties his fancy wrapper

And the son of a poor person will use only a loin as a wrap

Ifá's message for Ojomida

Alapamoru's son

When you face serious health challenges

And he was waiting for the day that he will be healthy again

He was advised to offer ebo

fulfilled

What were the things they were going to use to ward off death hanging over Ojomida

200 hoes and 200 dress spinners

Let the switch continue to move sideways

The day of my departure has not yet come

That no one regrets over me

ÒYÈKÚ ÒGÚNDÀ VERSE 14

Ire ni o wa isa lodede

Dia fun Alapa-Moru

Omo ateni legelege fori sapeji omi

Ti nraye re lainiiku

Ebo ni won ni ko waa se

O gb'ebo, o ru'bo

Ojo ti mo da ee pe

E ma wule salore e mi

Omo eku ee dagba

Omo eku o setan ti yoo kuu

Omo eja ee dagba

Omo eja o setan ti yoo kuu

Omo eye ee dagba

Omo eye o setan ti yoo kuu

Omo eran ee dagba

Omo eran o setan ti yoo kuu

Ojo ti mo da ee pe

E ma wule salore e mi o

Omo o mi ee dagba

Emi ee setan ti ng o kuu

Translation

The cricket does not dig a hole inside the house

Ifá's message for Alapamori

The one who spread his rug delicately near the stream

When goes to the life of longevity

He was advised to offer ebo

fulfilled

My time on Earth had not yet expired

That no one regrets over me

The rat has not grown to maturity

The rat is not ready to die yet

That no one regrets over me

The fish has not yet reached maturity

The fish is not yet ready to die

That no one regrets over me

The bird has not yet reached maturity

The bird is not yet ready to die

That no one regrets over me

The beast has not yet reached maturity

The beast is not yet ready to die

That no one regrets over me

My children are not mature yet

I'm not ready to die yet

PROPHECY

14. Ifá says that he will never die young. However, he will have to offer ebo and feed Egungun regularly. Ifa advises you to offer ebo with three roosters and money. You also need to feed Egungun with lots of bean milk, moinmoin, lots of cornmeal, Eko and lots of Atori switches.

ÒYÈKÚ ÒGÚNDÀ VERSE 15

Igbo ewuro ni o lomi

Odan lomi re e wa

Dia fun Esuu-la-mokun

Tii somo Olofin

O dagba-dagba o nwoko imoran ya kiri

Ebo ni won ni ko waa se

O gb'ebo, o ru'bo

Esuu-la-mokun omo Olofin

Esuu-la-mokun o dalaje

Esuu la mokun omo Olofin o

Esuu-la-mokun o d'oloko

Esuu la mokun omo Olofin o

Esuu-la-mokun o d'olomo

Esuu la mokun omo Olofin o

Translation

The forest of bitter license trees has no water

The water is in the savannah zone

Ifá's message for Esuu-la-mokun

Olofin's daughter

When she grew up and went looking for an unemployed husband

She was advised to offer ebo

she obeyed

Esuu-la-mokun the daughter of Olofin

Esuu-la-mokun you have become a rich woman

Esuu-la-mokun the daughter of Olofin

She has received the blessing of a compatible spouse

Esuu-la-mokun who has received the blessing of many children

Esuu-la-mokun the daughter of Olofin

She has received the blessing of her personal property

Esuu-la-mokun the daughter of Olofin

She has received the blessing of all the wrath of life

Esuu-la-mokun the daughter of Olofin

PROPHECY

15. Ifa says that there is a woman very close to you who is having trouble securing a compatible partner. Ifá says that it is ifa himself who will guide this woman in order to fulfill choosing her own partner in her life. Ifá advises this woman to offer ebo with four chickens and money. You also have to feed Ifa with two rats, two fish and a chicken.

ÒYÈKÚ ÒGÚNDÀ VERSE 16

Ito oganjo nii m'eyin jo ejo

Dia fun Oori patako

Tii somoye inu oko

Ebo ni won ni ko waa se

O koti ogbonyin sebo

Nje awo Oriri ko tawa o

Awa kii sawo lalai si fila

Awo oriri ko tawa

Awa kii sawo lalai si gele

Awo Oriri ko tawa

Translation

Urine from the depths of the night resembles the movement of a snake

The Ifá message for the giant Oori tree

The owner of agricultural land

He was advised to offer ebo

He refuses to comply

Our practice is not that of Oori

We will never practice AWO without removing the caps

Our practice is not that of Oori

We will never practice AWO without removing the wear from the head

Our practice is not that of Oori

PROPHECY

16. Ifá says that at any time you want to pray to Ifa and all the other divinities, you must make sure that you take off your cap and make sure that everyone around you has removed their hats and caps. Ifá says that if someone puts something to cover his head during the prayer, such a prayer will not be accepted. Ifa advises you to offer ebo with two rats, two fish and money. You also need to feed Ifa with two rats and two fish.

ORISHA ÒGÚN

CHAPTER 3

ÒYÈKÚ ÒSÁ o RIKÚSA

```
    +
O   O
I   O
I   O
I   O
```

I PRAY:

Òyèk ú Rikúsa kukute kukú A dífá fún Ògún ati Òṣósii. Dariko Òyèk ú Sa ká fírè fún Oya, Òrúnmìlà Adifáyoko ala dafá Awo ala dafá otoké toyo inyan méjì inyan lowó Osa nito le suṣu ko má ndi ko likú edan atoke toye orugbo ikóodide, Àkúko pupa Elebo.

PROVERBS:

- All that glitters is not gold.
- You do not want to throw in one day, what they owe you seven days ago.
- Do not despise the one who cast you out of misery.
- The vein one wants to be a dried fig, before it has been ripened

BORN:

- Agoi (Babalú Ayé female)

BRAND

- Eegún's Obsessor of Influence.
- War.

SIGNALIZE

- Disrespect.
- Spiritual phenomena.

IFÁ SPEAKS

- That the person does not meet any Saint
- That he lives in the middle with another and that does not suit him
- Of a family member who suffered from legs in life and used crutches
- That the Awo of this Ifá does not respect Òrúnmìlà, usually he continues to live the same life he lived before doing Ifá and in the end, he lives among shit
- Of spiritual phenomena. The person believes he sees things that walk, speak, carry and fall by virtue of his thoughts, in short, fantastic things that are transformed into whims of his mind.
- That the person, whether man or woman, marries the person who calls their attention, according to their mental

fantasies, without analyzing if that conjugation really suits them and then failure comes and even death
- To paint the house white and have it clean and tidy so that Ọbàtàlá can visit it and give you the luck that it has for you.
- That you cursed a ọmọ de Ṣàngó and that curse turned against you.
- E that the person lives under the influence of an obsessor Eegún that leads him to do everything he should not, it is necessary to make him Paraldo with what Orúnmìlà indicates.
- You have to see that Elégbà wants it not to destroy the house, if it has not already been done.
- That the person does not treat the Bàbálawos with the respect they deserve and that delays him
- That in the house two people fight for the possession of money or for the possession of the house. Make Ẹbọ so you don't lose.
- That if he becomes proud and lacking, he will be thrown out of his house
- That the person wants to get money to do something he has in hand
- That there will be a dead man in the corner of your house.
- That you are starving and have cried these days, you have no one to help you

PROHIBITIONS

- Okra is not eaten
- You can't live half with anyone

RECOMMENDATIONS

- You should not get wet in rainwater and much less if you are the son of Ọbàtàlá
- Must wear white and always be clean
- Beware of death suddenly, go to the doctor to get checked
- Make Paraldo with what Òrúnmìlà indicates
- Do not be ungrateful with what they do you good so that they do not curse you
- Don't get upset and pay Ṣàngó what he owes you
- Beware of disgust and blood on your way
- Put a bunch of Bananas in Ṣàngó and cover it with Alamo leaves for 9 days in which the Àṣeré will touch it, so that it covers everything bad that you have in your way.
- Avoid crossing the sea and the river and if you plan to go to the field, do Ẹbọ first to avoid setbacks.
- Do not curse as it will reach you
- Be careful that you can be killed in the corner of your house

EWÉ ODÙ ỌYÈKÚ ỌSÁ

Alamo

For more information see: Encyclopedia of Ifá herbs by Marcelo Madan

PATAKI LISTING

1. The war of Èṣù and Ṣàngó
2. Phenomenal spirits are born
3. Ọbàtàlá and Ṣàngó
4. Darico's Ẹbọ

5. When Darico was disrespectful to Òrúnmìlà

WORKS WITH ÒYÈKÚ ÒSÁ

ẸBỌ: Akoidíe, Àjapá, Oguedé apple trees, red beans

Three people fight for money and no one can get involved, not the family or justice. ẸBỌ: Àkúko méjì, Abeboadié méjì ... the animals are not killed until they win.

ẸBỌ to take that disputed money:

Àkúko méjì, adié méjì, these animals will remain alive until they obtain what they want and then they wonder what to do with them.

Ẹbọ: Işi's tail, a güiro, Àkúko, adié, Işi's crap and $ Right.

Ẹbọ: An Àkúko, a méta corn cob, an adié Dúdú, eku, eja, and $ Derecho. ẸBỌ:

16 Parrot Feathers.

Ẹbọ: ẹtù méjì.

Ẹbọ: He goes to the street right away. The one with the 16

Parrot Feathers, 16 of ẹiyelé are added.

Ẹbọ: Roasted yam, enough Epó, to later give it to the warriors, also take ẹiyelé sometimes. Owó la Méta

ẸBỌ: Àkúko méjì, Abeboadié méjì... animals are not killed until I win. ẸBỌ to take that disputed money:

Àkúko méjì, adié méjì, these animals will remain alive until they obtain what is desired and

then he wonders what to do with them.

Ẹbọ:

Cola de Işi, a güiro, Àkúko, adié, crap from Işi and $ Right.

Ẹbọ:

One Àkúko, méta corn cob, one adié Dúdú, eku, eja, and $ Derecho.

ẸBỌ:

16 parrot feathers. Ẹbọ: ẹtù méjì. Ẹbọ: He goes to the street right away. The one with the 16 Parrot Feathers, 16 of ẹiyelé are added.

Ẹbọ: Roasted yam, a lot of Epó, to later give it to the warriors, also take ẹiyelé sometimes. Owo the goal

All that glitters is not gold"

Ẹbọ:

Akoidíe, Àjapá, Oguedé manzanos, Red beans

Three people fight for money and no one can get involved, neither the family nor the justice system.

Ẹbọ:

Àkúko méjì, Abebo adie méjì... animals are not killed until I win

Ẹbọ to catch that disputed money:

Àkúko méjì, adie méjì, these animals will stay alive until they get what they want and then they wonder what is done with them.

Ẹbọ:

Işi cola, a güiro, Àkúko, adie, Işi crap and $

Ẹbọ:

One Àkúko, méta corn cob, one adie dudu, eku, eja, and $

You are starving, you have cried these days, you say you have no one to help you

Ẹbọ:

16 Parrot Feathers. Ẹbọ: ẹtu méjì. Ẹbọ: He goes to the street right away. The one with the 16 Parrot Feathers, 16 of ẹiyelé are added.

Do not make a partnership with anyone who is you who goes wrong. You are late on this matter

Intorí Arayé: Àkúko. Intorí Aikú: Àgbo el Ẹbọ

Who he hangs out with does not suit him, he must be thrown out of the house, because it will bring bad consequences

Ẹbọ:

Roasted yam, a lot of Epó, to later give it to the warriors, also take ẹiyelé sometimes. Owó the Metatutista.

ÒYÈKÚ RI KU SÁ PÀTAKI 1 "THE WAR OF EṢU AND ṢANGO"

Pàtaki

Once Ṣàngó had a war with Èṣù's son, the latter was always armed because he wanted to kill Ṣàngó wherever he was found. One day when Ṣàngó was walking he met Èṣù's son and he took out his weapon to kill him, and Ṣàngó who was unarmed had to run for his life, Èṣù's son did not want to miss the opportunity and ran after him , when Ṣàngó managed to get ahead of him and had a great advantage, he saw a Poplar tree and climbed on it, and hid among the branches, when Èṣù's son reached the bush he did not see Ṣàngó anywhere and was amazed because He did not understand how Ṣàngó had disappeared before his eyes, Ṣàngó took the opportunity to fall on him and knocked him face down on the ground and thus he was able to defeat him.

Note:

That is why the Poplar leaves that are chosen for the saint or other work for 51ase are those that are 51ase up, using those that are 51ase down for other bad work and Itútù.

ÒYÈKÚ RI KU SÁ PÀTAKI 2 "THE SPIRITS PHENOMENA THE SPIRITUAL PLASMA IS BORN"

I PRAY:

Agoi ọmọde Asójaanú ọmọ litase tasa niwa gutu azon Obìrin odara ebe ja wo ọkọnrin opolopo owó alagba agba ọkọnrin odara nanu iya gbogbo Asójaanú femimo oteri ba ṣo kuku to nilé zambeto da jo ni Bàbá Eegún oro awo Ikofá Agoi Aikú Lodafún Òrúnmìlà káfírèfún Asójaanú ikú.

Ẹbọ:

7 Yam, 1 bottle of òtí Kànà, Àkúko, 1 Àjapá, 1 Àgbo, 1 pipa, áṣo timbè lara.

Iyere:

Agoi wiywbé, Agoi keiyewé

Bàbá Eegún enIfá Aikú

Pàtaki

On this road Asójaanú, Soyi and Nami had a very beautiful daughter who rejected all the suitors who wanted to marry her, because she only wanted a man who matched her in bodily beauty and luxury. This maiden was called Agoi and she sold emiwó, erú and adalú in front of the palace of her father from Soyi Cajuá. One day she saw a man coming from afar whose image seduced her, because this stranger was slender and wrapped in rich dresses, she was waiting for him impatiently, far from her work and she went in to get ready a little, calling all her brothers and her father, her mother and said to them: With that man I will marry:

Agoi prepared everything that same day and got married, as was customary since she could not sleep in her house and she went with the man to her land. After long hours of travel, Agei asked her husband, where are we going? He said to the middle of the earth and they continued walking, a little later a voice was heard on the mountain that said: Debli-Godó, give me your clothes. Agei's husband undressed easily before the eyes of his terrified wife who saw that that beautiful man was nothing more than a spirit, the being was left alone as a candle of bright light, without head, arms, or foot. As she was sworn in as a child in Zamgbete, Eegún arará was filled with courage and decided to reach the end of her journey. They crossed a river of strange waters where many fabrics of sumptuous colors walked and talked like men, they were Eegún, Agei came out of his astonishment and said: How many strange things, then he saw a fetal boy who walked inside his jar with a crown of feathers la lerí (was seri-Antonia Gervacio). When night fell, she saw another major sight, an Àkúko wearing pants and smoking a pipe, it was the spirit of Òsányin.

The spirit of her husband told her: Never tell, because you will die. When she arrived at her husband's house, she was received by even stranger beings who walked by virtue of her thought, they found her too emaciated to sacrifice her to Alosin and left her for seven days so that she could recover.

ÒYÈKÚ RI KU SÁ PÀTAKI 3 "ÒBÀTÁLA AND ṢÀNGÓ"

Ẹbọ: Ìkóodide, Abebo adie méjì, krin of horse, and crap

Pàtaki

It says that Dariko went to Òrúnmìlà's house and did Ẹbọ with all the effects and then whitewashed his house. Being one day out of it, a great storm appeared and caught him in water in the street and he took shelter in Òbàtála's house, all wet. He took pity on her and gave her clothes. Dariko improved the entrance of him and went into horse trading and dealing, he was very lucky. One day Òrúnmìlà came and Dariko, giving importance to himself on his horse, instead of getting off to greet Òrúnmìlà, he greeted him on the run. Òrúnmìlà, indignant, sent Elégbà to destroy everything completely and Dariko was left in misery.

ÒYÈKÚ RI KU SÁ PÀTAKI 4 "THE ẸBỌ OF DARICO"

Pàtaki

Darico went to Òrúnmìlà's house and made Ẹbọ with: ẹiyelé funfun, shell and $4.20, with the efún he whitewashed his house. Shortly after, Òbàtála went for a walk and in the middle of the road a storm surprised him, having to take shelter in Darico's house, becoming very happy to see such a white house.

After a while Darico arrived under a torrential downpour and Òbàtála gave him clothes and àşe.

From that moment Darico became a horse dealer, making him happy.

ÒYÈKÚ RI KU SA PÀTAKI 5 "WHEN DARICO WAS DISRESPECTFUL TO ÒRÚNMÌLÀ"

Pàtaki

It happened that once Darico met Òrúnmìlà on the road and instead of greeting him with respect, he said indifferently, continuing his march, "Iború, Iboya, Iboşìşé".

Then Òrúnmìlà later met Èṣù and told him how wrong Darico had behaved with him.

Soon after, Èṣù made all Darico's businesses go bankrupt, seeing his arrears, he returned to Òrúnmìlà's house to clean himself. Òrúnmìlà asked him for the Ẹbọ horse crap and to paint the front of his house with it, Òbàtála came out again and noticing that the day was cloudy because Darico's house was very stinky he did not enter.

And since then Darico lives among the filth.

Èṣù

CHAPTER 4

TRADITIONAL IFA ÒYÈKÚ ÒSÁ

(OYEKU TEKU ASA; OYEKU WOLE TOSA; ÒYEKU GASA)

ÒYÈKÚ ÒSÁ VERSE 1

Bee ni ko ni kese

Amukuuru lo gesin

Bee ni o rese bo bata

Ire to ni kese to rese bo bata

Bee ni o resin amugun

Dia fun Oyeku

Ti yoo gesin rele Osa o

Ebo ni won ko waa se

O gb'ebo, o ru'bo

Translation

The mini bug rides on a horse but has no rein

And Amukuru bug rides on a horse, but he has no clapper

The cricket that has both clapper and feet to carry boot

He doesn't have a horse to ride

Ifá's message for Oyeku

When riding a horse to Osa's house

She was advised to offer ebo

fulfilled

Oyeku has ridden a horse to Osa's house

We are all going to transact our Ifa businesses on horses

PROPHECY

1- Ifá says that he foresees the blessing of prosperity and financial success for this person. You have to be initiated in Ifa and follow Ifa's advice at all times. Ifá advises that person to offer ebo with a mature goat, three pigeons, three guinea fowl, three hens and money. You also need to feed Ifa with a chicken.

ÒYÈKÚ ÒSÁ VERSE 2

Oyeku wokun wosa

Oyekuu won lo ree wosa

Ariwo Saalesaale

Dia fun Oju

Ti nlo wobi rere loo joko

Ebo ni won ko waa se

O gb'ebo, o ru'bo

Oju wobi rere jokoo o

Aguntan opopo wobi to tutu se falala

Translation

Oyeku explore the sea and the lagoon

Oyeku has gone to look for Osa

There is crisis and chaos

Ifá's message for Oju the eye

When you go to find a comfortable place to sit

She was advised to offer ebo

she obeyed

Oju has found a comfortable place to sit

The sheep of sight had searched for a comfortable place to enjoy his life

PROPHECY

2- Ifá says that she foresees the peace and tranquility of this user. Ifá advises that person to offer ebo in order to find a comfortable place to settle. The ebo materials here include:

four pigeons, four chickens, and money. There is a need for this person to feed Ifa with a matured sheep.

ÒYÈKÚ ÒSÁ VERSE 3

Oluwo asa o gb'aja

Awodi o pa saa gb'eyin nikun adie

Agba to nfinu sika

To nfita sotito

Bo ba pe titi

Oun ti yoo bini o gbalai bi'ni

Dia fun Aseke

Tii s'obinrin Orisa

Ebo ni won ko waa se

O koti ogbonyin sebo

Eyin o ri Aseke o

Bo ti da ise sile fun Oosa

Bo ti da ise sile fun Oosa

Translation

The hawk can't catch a dog

And the 6Orobl cannot catch an egg in the stomach of a bird.

An old man who is evil internally, but who shows justice outwardly

Sooner or later nemesis rob catch up with him

Ifá's message for Aseke, the lies

Orissa's wife

She was advised to offer ebo

she did not comply

Can't you see how Aseke

As a roblema created by Orisa

PROPHECY

3. Ifa says that there is a need for this person to feed Obatala with 16 snails, EFUN and Osun. Ifá warns that this person never lie or show evil.

ÒYÈKÚ ÒSÁ VERSE 4

Omo olohun pii nle

Omo olowo teere lori esin

Dia fun Oyeku

To nlo ree gasa

Ebo ni won ko waa se

O gb'ebo, o ru'bo

Igba Oyeku gasa

La di Olokun la di Onide

Translation

The son of an ordinary person jumped to the ground

And a rich person's son jumped on a horse

Ifá's message for Oyeku

When you gonna ride on Asa

She was advised to offer ebo

fulfilled

When Oyeku mounted Asa

That was the time we were blessed with Okun beads and brass ornaments

PROPHECY

4. Ifá says that he foresees the prosperity of this user. Ifa advises you to offer ebo with two pigeons, two chickens, four rats, four fish and money. You also have to feed Ifa with a chicken, two rats and two fish.

ÒYÈKÚ ÒSÁ VERSE 5

Sugbudun

Dia fun Oyeku

Nijo to nlo weri Osa lodo

Ebo ni won ko waa se

O gb'ebo, o ru'bo

Sugbundun

Oyeku weri Osa o

Sugbundun

Translation

Sugbudun

It was the AWO that cast Ifa for Oyeku

When he goes to wash the Ori de Osa in the stream

He was advised to offer ebo

fulfilled

Sugbudun

Oyeku washes Osa's head

Sugbudun

PROPHECY

5. Ifá says that he foresees the prosperity of this user. This person has to wash his Ori from him with a special soap made from Awede leaves and pig's blood. This person has to go to a stream to wash the Ori from him.

ÒYÈKÚ ÒSÁ VERSE 6

Apa Aja

Roro Agbo

Emi o mo oun ti won di legbinrin

Dia fun Oyeku

Ti nrele Osa baba re lo ree sawo

Ebo ni won ko waa se

O gb'ebo, o ru'bo

Oyeku Teku Asa o

Esin lao ma gun sawo

Translation

The four arms of a dog

And the neck of a ram

I don't know what they prepared for us inside the sack

Ifá's message for Oyeku

When he goes to his father's house in Osa Ifa mission

She was advised to offer ebo

fulfilled

Oyeku went to cast Ifa from Osa

We are all going to ride a horse to transact our Ifa business

PROPHECY

6. The person who wants to go on a trip. This person is going to bring success and prosperity back from this journey. Ifa advises you to offer ebo with two pigeons, two hens, two roosters and money. You also need to feed Ifa with four rats and four fish and feed the spirit of his father, as appropriate.

ÒYÈKÚ ÒSÁ VERSE 7

Oju ni sake

Awo ni jojo

Alabenbe nii fo balabala ni MÒgún

Dia fun Orunmila

Ifa nsunkun alairi eru je

Ebo ni won ko waa se

O gb'ebo, o ru'bo

N o si kofa

N o si reru je o

Ewe sayoo temi

N kasai reru je o

Translation

eyes show beauty

And the skin shows brilliance

The mini bat flies clumsily inside the Ògún shrine

Ifá's message for Orunmila

When lamenting his inability to make a profit from his Ifa business

She was advised to offer ebo

fulfilled

I will take Ifa study more seriously

And I will have profit from my Ifa business

Sayo sheets have authorized

That I will have profit from my Ifa business

PROPHECY

7. Ifa urges this person to take the IFA study more seriously. Ebo materials here are: two pigeons, two guinea fowl and money. You have to pound Sayo leaves with soap and use the mixture in the bathroom regularly. Doing this will bring you success.

ÒYÈKÚ ÒSÁ VERSE 8

Papajaja aakara

Dia fun Orunmila

O nloo gbe Fekunwe niyawo

Ebo ni won ko waa se

O koti ogbonyin sebo

Igba ti e ri Fekunwe naa

E se bi olomo ni o?

Translation

The old worn pumpkin

He launched Ifá for Orunmila

When he is going to marry his wife Fekunwe

He was advised to offer ebo

The way you have seen Fekunwe

Do you think he is blessed to have children

PROPHECY

8. Ifa says that there is a woman in this sign revealed that a person intends to marry. Ifá warns that this woman does not have the blessing of having children from heaven. Anyone who marries her should not expect a child from her. If this person doesn't want any child from the woman any longer, then they can go ahead and get married. But if the man is interesting, having more children than the woman is not his choice.

ÒYÈKÚ ÒSÁ VERSE 9

Ki nseso fun e

Eso onibuje ko ka'adun

Ibi orun lo mo

Dia fun Orunmila

Tii somo Elegbaa Eyin

Dia fun Opolo

Tii somo alawoo torotoro

Ebo ni won ni ki won waa se

Orunmila nikan ni nbe leyin ti nsebo

Eyin o wo eyin ara Orunmila

Bo ti wa d'eyin ara Opolo

Translation

Makeup Design on my body

For me the makeup design on your body

The tattoo bushing makeup design does not last up to a year

Cannot be more than five days

Ifá's message for Orunmila

Who was inflicted with 2000 points and scabies

And also for Opolo the toad

The owner of the snake as a pledge

They were advised to offer ebo

Only Orunmila fulfilled

Can't you see the locations and scabies on Orunmila's body

As they now become the scab and stain on Opolo's body, the toad

PROPHECY

9. Ifa says that there is someone in this sign revealed that she needs to offer ebo against the disease of the body. Ifá warns this person to offer ebo with three roosters, three hens and money. You also have a garment that looks like the skin of a snake. You also have to offer this syrup as ebo. There is also the need to pound sheets bushing with the soap for this person to use to take to your bathroom. Ifa also warns this person to be careful not to come into contact with and inherit diseases from other people.

Seso fan mi

ÒYÈKÚ ÒSÁ VERSE 10

Aguntan gboke odo

Senu bonbo ba won lÒgún lo

Dia fun Oyeku pelu Osa

Won ngbogún roke odo

Ebo ni won ko waa se

O gb'ebo, o ru'bo

Arogún lenii o

Ògún ti lo o

Oye mi o sa o

Ògún ti lo o

Translation

The sheep crossed the stream

And opened his dull mouth to chase away crises

Ifá's message for Oyeku and Osa

They're gonna make war across the stream

They were advised to offer ebo

fulfilled

We have encountered the current crisis

And the crisis was gone

Oyemi Osa or

The crisis was gone

PROPHECY

10. Ifá advises that person to offer the ebo of victory. This person is going to see something scary but you are going to

get over it. Ifá advises that person to offer ebo with a matured male goat and money. You also have to give gifts to Gangan drummers. Ifa assures this person that crises will disappear in a single day.

ÒYÈKÚ ÒSÁ VERSE 11

Adeyeri leni a ba bu

Adetutu leni a ba foro lo

Eni moran tan di Olodumare

A jaye Ifa gbendengbenden bi eni nlayin

Dia fun Aikulola

Tii somo Elese-Mawi

Eyi ti o ni ori Iyin

To jori ase lo ni

Ebo ni won ko waa se

O gb'ebo, o ru'bo

Nje ayikan nlaa y'ayin

Enu tee m yin mi o

E ma mu'hun pada

Ayinkan laa yayin o

Translation

Adeyeri is someone we should insult

And Adetutu is someone you should consult

Anyone who knows everything has become Olodumare

You will be able to enjoy the life of Ifá has someone leaks pure honey

Ifá's message for Aikulola

Elese-Mawe's son

The one without Ori of revaluation

But Ori of contempt

He was advised to offer ebo

fulfilled

It is with satisfaction that we praise Ayin

The mouth has been used to praise me

Don't change your voice

It is with satisfaction that we praise Ayin

PROPHECY

11. Ifa says that there is a need for this person to feed her Ori so that people can appreciate all her efforts. Ifá says that all his good deeds were viewed with disdain. Ifá advises that person to offer ebo with three roosters, three hens, three bottles of honey and money. You also have to feed your Ori and feed

Ifa accordingly. Ifá advises that person to chew Ayin chewing stick regularly.

ÒYÈKÚ ÒSÁ VERSE 12

Oyeku saa

Dia fun Olo

Tii nbe laarin ota

Ebo ni won ko waa se

O gb'ebo, o ru'bo

Ko pe, ko jinna

E wa ba ni laruuse Ògún

Translation

Oyeku saa

Ifá's message for Olo, the grinding stone

When she was in the midst of enemies

She was advised to offer ebo

she obeyed

In a short time, not far

Join us in the midst of all life Ire

PROPHECY

12. Ifá says that this person will overcome all enemies. This person has to feed the Ori of the first male child of hers. Ifá advises that person to offer ebo with three roosters, three hens and money. You also have to feed your child's Ori, as appropriate.

ÒYÈKÚ ÒSÁ VERSE 13

Oye tenu bosa

Koo kewe sodi

Dia fun Ebe

Ti n loo gbesu niyawo

Ebo ni won ko waa se

O gb'ebo, o ru'bo

Igba ebe gbesu niyawo

Igba omo lo mu bo

Translation

Hey tenu bosa

koo kewe sodi

The Ifá message for the farm heap

When she is going to marry the wife thread

She was advised to offer ebo

fulfilled

When the farm heap married yam as a wife

He came home with 200 children

PROPHECY

13. Ifá advises that person to offer ebo in order to receive the blessing of a compatible spouse. Ebo materials here: three chickens, four rats, four fish for the male and three roosters, four rats, four fish for the female.

ÒYÈKÚ ÒSÁ VERSE 14

Koto-koto-koto

Dia fun Adaba susu

Ti ngbiogún relu Asa

Ebo ni won ko waa se

O gb'ebo, o ru'bo

Adaba susu ti ngbÒgún relu Asa

Ifa ti ni ko sewu o

Translation

Koto-koto koto-

Ifá's message for Adaba, the dove

When he goes on a military campaign to the land of the falcon

He was advised to offer ebo

fulfilled

The dove that will make war in the land of the falcon

Ifá says that there is nothing to fear

PROPHECY

14. Ifa assures this person that you will have to overcome. You are afraid and you have premonitions. There is no need for this person to fear. You will go and come back safely. Ifá advises that person to offer ebo with a matured male goat and money.

ÒYÈKÚ ÒSÁ VERSE 15

Gbongbo lokun

Gbongbo losa

Dia fun Ogodo

Tii somo Onipapo-iko-ni-Ejin

Ogodo boo ti nrubo ola

Bee ni koo maa rubo tomo

Translation

gbongbo lokun

gbongbo slab

Ifá's message for Ogodo, the silk cotton

Onipapo Oleji's son

He was advised to offer ebo

she obeyed

Ogodo are being offered the ebo of prosperity

Also present the ebo to procreate

PROPHECY

15. Ifá says that this person has to offer ebo for both motherhood and prosperity together. Ifá says that the two will come to this person together. Ifá advises that person to offer ebo with two pigeons, two chickens, four rats, four fish and money.

ÒYÈKÚ ÒSÁ VERSE 16

Eekan okuna abita parapara jana

Dia fun Orunmila

Ifa nloo tun ahoro baba re se

Ebo ni won ko waa se

O gb'ebo, o ru'bo

Ifa ni yoo so ahoro dile

Oosa ni yoo so odide doja

Ifa ni yoo so ahoro dile

Translation

Eekan okuna abita parapara jana

Ifá's message for Orunmila

Going to repair his abandoned ancestral home

She was advised to offer ebo

fulfilled

Ifa will turn an abandoned place into a home of life

Orisa will light a living room with a market

Ifa will turn an abandoned place into a home of life

PROPHECY

16. Ifá says that the ancestral home of this person has to be abandoned. There is a need for this person to feed the site of this house in her case. You also have to feed the ancestral divinities of your paternal lineage

CHAPTER 5

VOCABULARY AND DEFINITIONS

WHAT FOR PROFESSIONAL ETHICS, EVERYTHING MUST KNOW BABALAWO

1. rom memory, a large part of the Ifá literary corpus.

    a. Masterfully manipulate the instruments of the oracle of divination.

2. Must be a well-versed interpreter, of the metaphorical language typical of ancestral literature.

3. Know exhaustively, the fauna and flora of your country and the therapeutic and magical utility of a large number of plants.

4. Know the fundamental ideograms (Odù de Ifá) and the incantations inserted in them.

5. You must constantly raise your level of theological and scientific information.

"In Ifá there is not everything, in Ifá everything fits".

This serves as a universal data bank where all existing existential events are stored, classified in the Ifá code.

"The true way to know nothing is to want to learn everything at once"

Ògbè Òdí

SOME ESSENTIAL ELEMENTS FOR THE INTERPRETATION IN THE ACT OF DIVINATION.

Ká firè fún ----- Finish comforting.

A dífá fún ------ He was in search of divination. Lodá fún ------- You will perform the divination.

Mo firè fún ---- Òṣà that we must take as a behavioral reference (her example or behavioral pattern in history or pataki that she refers to).

Abo fún -------- Who is close to the consulted.

Ajogún --------- Bad spiritualities (Death, illness, loss, etc.)

Ayanmó (Añamó) --- Destiny.

Áyewo (Ayeo)   Hex.

Ké fèrí lorí………..Incredulous.

Kán Kán lòní -------- Quickly, today, right now. Kí nnkan má ṣe ---- Protect from evil forces.

Kó le ni ó díwo (Koleniodio) --- It shouldn't be occupying you all the time. Jálè   Complete.

Mo jálè ---- Continue further.

Kòtó jálè --- It is insufficient, follow it or complete it.

Bé ko yes ---- Begging for something that is not there (is something missing?). Laarí iṣé òrìṣà? ------ Is a job with Òṣà important?

Ní torí, Intórí ------- Because of.

Lésè -------- At the foot of, follow the trail. **Lówó** ------- at the hands of.

Igbó -------- Forest, mone, manigua.

Ode..........Hunter.

Dáfá..........Divination.

SOME IRÉ E IBI (OSOBO) IMPORTANT RÉ

Iré aikú -------------------- Health benefit and long life

Iré àşẹ́ gun ---------------- Benefit to win or conquer

Iré àşẹ́ gun ọtá ------------ Benefit from defeating enemies

Iré aya --------------------- Profit from a wife

Iré deedeewántòloòkun -Benefit of coming and going to the sea, fishermen, merchants

Iré omaa --------------------Intelligence benefit

Iré ìrìnkiri (inikini) -------- Travel benefit

Iré lésè eegún ------------ Benefit at the foot of the dead

Iré lésè ẹléda ------------- Benefit at the foot of the creator

Iré mérin layé ------------- Benefit that comes from the four parts of the world

Iré nlọlé siwaju -----------Benefit of improving by going to another land

Iré nşowó (Iré şowo) ---- Profit of doing business

OSOBO (IBI)

Afitibó --------- Unexpected death

Akóba --------- Unexpected punishment, an unforeseen evil

Àroye............Complaint

Àrùn (anu).......Disease

Ejo (eyo)..........Judgment

Ikú..............Death

Iyan (iña) ----- Hunger, famine, etc.

Òfo ------------- Irreconcilable loss, divorce, differences

Òràn (ona) ----Big problem

Ònà ------------ leather, bumps

ELEMENTS OF DIVINATION FOR COMMUNICATION WITH ORI (ÌBÒ)

Apadí (Akuadí) ---- Piece of porcelain slab, opposite to iré.

Apa (Akua) --------- Bull's-eye Seed (beat opponents).

Gúngún ------------- (death, deceased and conclude).

Igbin ---------------- Elongated snail (Ayé), means union.

Òtá ------------------ Small stone, longevity and war.

Owó ---------------- Double snail (cowries), currency, profit, acquire. Àwòran (Awona) --Small image of cloth or clay.

Àgbálùmò ----------.Caimito Seed, enjoy life

Efun ---------------- Cascarilla Ball, represents purity.

Eyin (eñi) ---------- Tooth of an animal, irreparable loss.

Isìn ----------------- Seed of the vegetable Cease, represents

Òrúnmìlà. Sáyò ----Guacalote seed, children and multiplicity of goods.

THREE ODÙ MAKE UP A "DETERMINING FIGURE OF IFÁ" WHEN THE ORACLE IS CONSULTED.

Considering that an event is given by a query that a person makes to the Ifá oracle. Three esoteric figures will be considered as a general rule, which from these events emerge to take into account:

The first reading is called: Odù Toyale Iwá (1680 stories; patakí; eses).

This Odù investigates and explains the destiny of the person and in turn represents their problems.

The second reading is called: Odù Okuta Kulá (1680 stories; patakí; eses).

This odù reaffirms in detail what is expressed in the Toyale, it speaks of the causes of the person's problem.

The third spread is called: Odù tomala belanşe (1680 stories; patakí; eses).

This odù reaffirms what was expressed by the previous ones and in turn provides various possible solutions to the person's problem.

There are also two others important odù to take into account: The Boyuto odù that is a kind of guardian odù of the Toyale odù and its writing results from the opposite writing of its encryption. And the odù Omotorun Iwa which is the odù formed by the union of the ends of the odù Toyale and the odù Tomala belanşe.

Each Odù is supposed to have 1680 of those stories related to him, and this along with those of the other odù, and each one of them is supposed to be known by the Bàbálawo who is the one who guesses and sacrifices, it is expected that he has it in memory, although we have not found any capable of that feat ......

Ifá Divination page 16 Willian Bascom (End of quote).

And we also find that some authors of works and writings specialized in these matters, agree with these criteria.

As each odù will have 1680 possible stories related to it, and with equal possibilities for all. Since the probabilities for the three odù are the same, that is; 256 times for each of the positions in a query to the Ifá oracle, that is: 256x256x256 = $(256)^3$ = 16, 777,216. (Sixteen million seven hundred seventy-seven thouSand two hundred sixteen). This means that there are the same possibilities for each event, if we divide 1 by the number of possibilities in the event, a figure will be so small that it tends to be considered or taken "as zero probability". It is evident that the result of this mathematical operation tells us that it is very unlikely that this same Ifá figure will be repeated for many consecutive events, taking into account that, for a certain figure, there is an intrinsically concatenation of ideas. Expressed and summarized in the odù of Ifá. For these reasons it is practically impossible for any human mind to be able to store, keep in its memory and at the same time process such a volume of information in a minimum of time or duration of a consultation, so that the consultant can be considered optimal conditions and ready, to give an adequate response to each of the issues that you face when consulting the Ifá oracle. Unless, you use modern search and information processing methods that are very fast and efficient. Only Olódùmaré its creator and Òrúnmìlà its interpreter, are able to achieve it efficiently. I suppose that a human being would have to live around 700 years of life, with a brain in optimal conditions to be able to achieve it.

Order of the hierarchy of animals

Ram------------------------Àgbò

Sheep----------------------Agutan

Male Goat-----------------Òbúko

Female Goat--------------Ewúre

Turtle----------------------Ajapa

Goose----------------------Ogbe

Peacoc.--------------------Tolo Tolo

Duck-----------------------Pepeiyé

Cock and Chicken---------kúko y Osadié

Hen-------------------------Adié

Pigeons--------------------Ẹiyelé

Guinea's Hen--------------Ẹtù

Quai------------------------Aparó

SOME EXPRESSIONS YORÙBÁ

Bẹ́ẹ̀ ni.- Yes.

Bẹ́ẹ̀ kó / ó ti.- No.

Ẹ̀ṣé.- thanks to you (to a superior or someone older than you).

Óṣe.- thank you (to someone younger than you).

Mo dupé.- I thank you.

To dupe.- We thank you.

Mo dupẹ́ pupò.- I thank you very much.

To dupẹ́ pupò.- We thank you very much.

Kò topic.- You are welcome / It is not mentioned / it is nothing.

Àlàáfíà.- Humbly greeting "be the Good", a way of greeting someone wishing them well at the same time.

Note: This greeting is best used between relatives or with people younger than you. It is not considered an acceptable greeting for an older person. In some cases, this may be the greetings used to greet and show respect to a priest of an Òrìsà, but when used in this way it is accompanied by a specific ritual gesture to distinguish it from a social greeting used between peers.

Ò dàbò.- Goodbye.

Note: This greeting is universally used among peers and is liked by the elderly.

Ẹ má bínú.- I'm sorry (to a superior or someone older than you).

Má bínú.- I am sorry (to a fellow man or someone younger than you).

Ẹ kò topic.- You are welcome / It is not mentioned / is nothing (to a superior or someone older than you).

Kò topic.- You are welcome / It is not mentioned / it is nothing (to a similar or someone younger than you).

¿Kí ni orúkọ rẹ.- What is your name?

Orúkọ mi ni.- My name is.

Note: It is generally considered improper to ask someone's name in Yoruba culture. The idea of introducing yourself greeting, but asking for your name is a concept of cultures foreign to the Yorùbá culture. The exception is when someone older than you ask for your name, this is considered acceptable.

Ẹ dide! - Get up (to a superior or someone older than you).

Ẹ jókòó.- Sit down (to a superior or someone older than you).

Dide! - Get up (to a peer or someone younger than you).

Jókòó.- Sit down (to a peer or someone younger than you).

Ẹ Madide! - Do not stand up (to a superior or someone older than you).

Ẹ má jókòó.- Do not feel (a superior or someone older than you).

Madide! - Do not stand up (to a peer or someone younger than you).

Má jókòó.- do not feel (like someone or someone younger than you).

Mo féràn rẹ.- I love him (a person, singular).

Mo féràn yin.- I love you (more than one person, plural).

Mo naa féràn rẹ.- I love him too (one person, singular).

Mo naa féràn yin.- (to more than one person, plural).

VOCABULARY USED

The list in the next section presents some forms commonly used in the Yorùbá language that are directly related to Òrìṣà or to the practice of Ifá.

Abo.- Female (indicates gender, does not speak of a woman).

Abòrìṣà.- A worshiper of the Òrìṣà, most often used in the Diaspora to signify someone who has received some basic initiations. This distinguishes that person from the rest of the community.

Àbọrú Àbọyè Àbọṣíṣẹ.- To be able to sacrifice / a prayer for the sacrifice to be heard To be able to sacrifice / a prayer for the sacrifice to be accepted To be able to sacrifice / a prayer for the sacrifice to manifest "Àbọrú, Àbọyè" is considered one of the appropriate greetings for a Babaláwo or Ìyánifá (initiated in Ifá). The priest will return the greeting of "Àbọṣíṣẹ." In many cases and the blessing will extend to the initiate return this greeting. This varies from priest to priest.

Àdìmú.- The food offered to the Ancestors and / or Òrìṣà.

Àdúrà.- Prayer.

Ako.- The male (indicates gender).

Àlàáfíà.- Greeting that means "be the Good", a way of greeting someone and wishing them well-being at the same time. See the important note below the greetings section.

Àṣẹ.- The life force; a common meaning; "The power to manifest" or "is for what".

Awo.- The mystery; a name for all the devotees of Òrìṣà; a name for an individual Òrìṣà priest; a term that identifies the religion of Ifá.

Àyèwò.- Research, often used instead of "Ibi" in divination to indicate the need to investigate the problems further.

Baba / Baba my.- Father / my father.

Babalóriṣá.- Male priest of Òrìṣà, often the father of spiritual children.

Cuje.- It is a fine rod made from the branches of the tree ("Rasca Barrigas")

Ẹbọ.- The sacrifice to offer. This can be used to indicate the offering of blood to the Òrìṣà although in the Diaspora this is often used as a term indicative of generally offering something to the Ancestors and the Òrìṣà.

Éérindínlógún.- The name of the sacred Oracle of the initiates of ìrìṣà.

It also refers to the sixteen cowries used during divination; the translation speaks "twenty minus four" which illustrates the Yorùbá way of calculating certain numbers.

Èèwò.- The taboo.

Ẹgbé.- Society or group of people, for example, Ẹgbé Ọ̀sun is a group of initiates of Ọ̀sun.

Èjè.- Blood.

Ẹmu opé.- The palm wine.

Epo Papua.- Red palm oil.

Ewé.- Leaves or herbs.

Ibi.- Bad luck, bad fortune.

Ìborì.- Ritually serve the head, praising and feeding one's Orí.

Idè.- The ankle bracelet, bracelet or necklace, refers to the sacred articles adorned with Òrìṣà beads, although it is more used in the Diaspora to indicate a bracelet of some kind.

Igbá.- Literally "the gourd", but it is often used to indicate a container filled with the sacred mysteries and the consecrated instruments of the Òrìṣà example, Igbá Ọsun is Ọsun, the sacred ritual container.

Ikin Ifá.- The sacred palm nuts used in the most important divination rituals.

Ilé.- Accommodation, house, describes a family from Òrìṣà.

Ìlèkè.- Literally "the beads" but it is often used to refer to the sacred necklaces adorned with Òrìṣà beads.

I'll go.- Good fortune, good luck.

Ìyá, Ìyá my.- Mother, my mother.

Ìyálórìṣà.- Priest woman of Òrìṣà, often the mother of spiritual children.

Obì abata.- The cola nut.

Obìrin.- Female or specifically a woman.

Odù Ifá.- The 256 signs or marks used in Ifá divination that represent the fundamental forces of creation in the universe, it is literally used as a reference to the body of Ifá.

Ọgbèrì.- Someone who has not received any kind of initiation into the mysteries of Òrìṣà, a novice.

Ọkùnrin.- The male, specifically a man.

Oloriṣa.- An initiate of the Òrìṣà man or woman. Sometimes this word is used to indicate someone who has been initiated into the mysteries of Òrìṣà but has not been spiritually initiated through the rites of consecration.

Olúwo.- In Ifá this term can be applied to an Ifá priest. The general meaning of the word indicates a person who teaches religion. It may, in some cases, indicate a certain line within the Ifá priesthood.

Omì tútù.- Fresh water

Omìèrò.- Water with consecrated herbs, "tranquilizing water".

Ọmọ.- The child, after spring. This can be used to refer to the biological years of spiritual children.

Ọ̀pèlè.- The Ifá divination chain.

Òrí.- White cocoa butter.

Oríkì.- Name of praise or story; sometimes used as an invocation to the matter of the Oríkì.

Orin.- The song.

Orógbó.- The bitter cola nut.

Ọṣẹ Dúdú / Ọṣẹ Aládin.- The black soap.

Ọtí.- A general word for spirits or wine.

Owó.- The money.

Oyin.- Honey.

SOME TERMS

Ajagún - The Yoruba term for warriors like the Orişa of protection.

Ajogún - The Yoruba term for denying forces.

Babalawo - The priest with a high degree of knowledge within the religious structure of Ifá.

Eegún - Hereditary entities.

Egúngún - The society within the Yoruba cultural structure that communes with and maintains the traditional directives of the ancestors.

Ehin Iwa - The Yoruba term for after life and reincarnation.

Elegun - Those initiated priests and priestesses who are possessed with the Orişa.

Enikejì - The Yoruba term for the guardian angel.

Eniyan Gidi - the Yoruba term for the authentic or true human being.

Idé - Sacred beads worn on the left wrist by Ifá devotees.

El llé-Ife - The ancient spiritual capital of the present Yoruba nation.

Ìmoyé - like wisdom

The Fá de Ìpìlé - The process of determining one's African origins, using the Ifá divination system.

Ìrùnmolè - The Yoruba term for divinities.

The Ìyáamí - A Yoruba term for witches (The Mothers).

The chestnut tree - The term applied to the societies of freedom established by the African captives escaped from the "New World". Technically, this word is Spanish and is used for sheep or cattle that have been lost.

Odù - The sacred text and the religious body of Ifá; that was named after the admired wife of Orunmila. Also, the term applied to the vessels containing the consecrated objects of the priests.

Odùdúwà - The patriarch of the current Yoruba nation that he established himself.

Ogbọní - The society of superiors within the present Yoruba cultural context, which maintains the connection with the Earth and the cultural forces of African society.

Olódùmarè - the Creator - God in the Yoruba cultural context.

O'lòrìşà - The Beginning of the priest or priestess within the Yoruba religious structure.

Òrìşà - The interpretation of Ifá, of energy forces that emanate from the Creator.

These evolutionary divinities are also declared anthropologically as cultural archetypes of light and avatars.

Òrúnmìlà - The prophet, established by the religious cult of Ifá.

MO FORI BALE IFÁ

ABOUT THE AUTHOR

Marcelo Madan born in 1944 in Santiago de Cuba. He comes from an Afro-Cuban family with deep religious roots. Consecrated in the orisha Ọbàtàlá since 1951. Awo of Orunmila, consecrated in Ifá as Babalawo by his godfather Ruben Pineda (Baba EjiÒgbè), since 1992. His paternal grandfather, Eligio Madan "Ifanlá" of slave parents brought from Africa and a native of Jovellanos in the province of Matanzas Cuba.

His maternal grandmother María Belén Hernández, a famous Iyalorisha from the city of Havana and consecrated in the orisha Ọbàtàlá. His father Eligio Madan Hernández Awo de Orunmila (Ògbè Owonrin) and consecrated in the orisha Oshun. His maternal grandmother, a famous Iyalorisha from the city of Santiago de Cuba. At the beginning of the forties and fifties Rosa Torrez "Shangó Gumí", who together with the famous babalorisha also son of Shangó Rinerio Pérez, Amada Sánchez and Aurora La Mar el Oriate Liberato and others, initiate the first settlement of orishas in that city; She is the granddaughter of Ma Braulia, a free woman who came from Africa. Veneranda Constanten, her mother, also consecrated in Ọbàtàlá (Ewin fún), she dedicated her whole life to religious work together with her mother, Rosa Torrez.

These are the deep ancestral roots of Marcelo Madan, which allowed them, through his consecration from an early age, to acquire the knowledge to carry out his religious literary works. And since then, he has become one of the most important researchers of the "lukumises" religion in Cuba, publishing dozens of books, among which are: the "Treaties of Ifá, Synthesis of the odu of Ifá, Orish Collections, The Oracles of the Orishas, Pocket Manual for Santeros, Meals and Adimú for the Saints among others.

Made in the USA
Columbia, SC
29 June 2024

37894816R00059